Money in The Bank

BY MARI SCHUH

MONEY & ME

Rourke
Educational Media
rourkeeducationalmedia.com

Before & After Reading Activities

Teaching Focus:

Teacher-child conversations: Teacher-child conversations play an important role in shaping what children learn. Practice this and see how these conversations help scaffold your student's learning.

Before Reading:

Building Academic Vocabulary and Background Knowledge

Before reading a book, it is important to set the stage for your child or student by using pre-reading strategies. This will help them develop their vocabulary, increase their reading comprehension, and make connections across the curriculum.

1. *Read the title and look at the cover. Let's make predictions about what this book will be about.*
2. *Take a picture walk by talking about the pictures/photographs in the book. Implant the vocabulary as you take the picture walk. Be sure to talk about the text features such as headings, Table of Contents, glossary, bolded words, captions, charts/ diagrams, or Index.*
3. Have students read the first page of text with you then have students read the remaining text.
4. *Strategy Talk – use to assist students while reading.*
   - *Get your mouth ready*
   - *Look at the picture*
   - *Think…does it make sense*
   - *Think…does it look right*
   - *Think…does it sound right*
   - *Chunk it – by looking for a part you know*
5. *Read it again.*

Content Area Vocabulary

Use glossary words in a sentence.

bank
banker
interest
loan
savings account
teller

After Reading:

Comprehension and Extension Activity

After reading the book, work on the following questions with your child or students in order to check their level of reading comprehension and content mastery.

1. *Describe the ways that banks help people with their money.* (Summarize)
2. *What is interest?* (Asking Questions)
3. *When a bank lends money to people, what is that money called?* (Asking Questions)
4. *If you could work at a bank, what job would you like to have and why?* (Text to Self Connection)

Extension Activity

Visit a bank! After reading this book, ask a parent or another trusted adult if you can visit a bank with them. Before you go, think about a few questions you might have. Also think about what you might see when you visit the bank. Pay close attention when you are there. Look around. Do you see any bank tellers? If so, how many do you see? Do you see other workers at the bank, such as bankers? If so, how many do you see? What other things do you notice at the bank?

Table of Contents

Rourke
Educational Media
rourkeeducationalmedia.com

Putting Money in the Bank

A check came in the mail. It's time to take it to the **bank**!

A check is a piece of paper that tells a bank to pay someone an amount of money.

Banks keep people's money safe.

A **teller** helps people who visit a bank. *"How can I help you?"*

Tellers help people put money into or take money out of their accounts.

People save money in a bank's **savings account**. The money earns **interest**.

Banks borrow money from savings accounts. They pay back the money plus interest. Interest is a fee paid to use someone else's money.

Borrowing Money

People borrow money from a bank.
They talk with a **banker**.

The bank lends them money. The money is called a **loan**. It helps people buy homes and cars.

A loan must be paid back within a certain amount of time.

People pay back the loan. They give the bank money every month.

Banks Help People

Banks help people save and spend.

People can take money out of their accounts by using an automated teller machine (ATM).

Banks help people reach their goals.

Photo Glossary

 **bank** (bangk): A business where people keep their money.

 **banker** (BANG-ker): A person who works at a bank and helps people with their accounts and loans.

 **interest** (IN-tur-ist): Money that people are paid for keeping money at a bank.

 **loan** (lohn): Money that is borrowed.

 **savings account** (SAY-vingz uh-KOUNT): Bank account in which money is stored.

 **teller** (TEL-ur): A bank worker who receives money from customers and pays out money to customers.

Index

Meet The Author!
www.meetREMauthors.com

Further Reading

Bellamy, Adam, *This Is My Bank*, Enslow Publishing, 2017.
Colby, Jennifer, *Banks*, Cherry Lake Publishing, 2018.
Schwartz, Heather E., *Bank Wisely*, Amicus, 2016.

Show What You Know

1. Who can help people borrow money from a bank?
2. What is a loan?
3. Name two ways banks can help people.

About the Author

Mari Schuh is the author of more than 300 nonfiction books for beginning readers, including many books about food, animals, and money. She lives with her husband in her hometown of Fairmont, Minnesota. You can learn more at her website: www.marischuh.com.

© 2019 Rourke Educational Media

www.rourkeeducationalmedia.com

PHOTO CREDITS: Cover ©dimdimich, ©Oksancia, Title Page ©dimdimich, Pages 3, 4, 6, 8, 10, 12, 14, 16, ©Oksancia, Pages 11 & 23 ©NicoElNino, Page 13 & 22 ©Weekend Images Inc., Pages 17 & 23 ©Dutko, Pages 11 & 22 ©choness, Pages 7 & 22 ©ultramarine5, Pages 9 & 23 ©YinYang, Page 5 ©bowdenimages, Page 15 ©sturti, Page 19 ©andresr, Page 21 ©Cecilie_Arcurs

Edited by: Keli Sipperley
Cover and Interior design by: Kathy Walsh

Library of Congress PCN Data
Money in the Bank / Mari Schuh
(Money & Me)
ISBN 978-1-64156-404-5 (hard cover)(alk. paper)
ISBN 978-1-64156-530-1 (soft cover)
ISBN 978-1-64156-655-1 (e-Book)
Library of Congress Control Number: 2018930426
Printed in the United States of America, North Mankato, Minnesota